VERSUS

MARVEL VS DC
A SUPERHERO SHOWDOWN

KENNY ABDO

Fly!
An Imprint of Abdo Zoom
abdobooks.com

abdobooks.com

Published by Abdo Zoom, a division of ABDO, P.O. Box 398166, Minneapolis, Minnesota 55439. Copyright © 2023 by Abdo Consulting Group, Inc. International copyrights reserved in all countries. No part of this book may be reproduced in any form without written permission from the publisher. Fly!™ is a trademark and logo of Abdo Zoom.

Printed in China.
102022
012023

Photo Credits: Alamy, Everett Collection, flickr, Getty Images, Shutterstock, ©Chris Hunkeler p.6/ CC BY-SA 2.0, ©Gary Dunaier p.9-10/ CC BY-SA 4.0, ©ocean yamaha p.17/ CC BY 2.0, ©Steve Baker p.20/ CC BY-ND 2.0
Production Contributors: Kenny Abdo, Jennie Forsberg, Grace Hansen
Design Contributors: Candice Keimig, Neil Klinepier, Laura Graphenteen

Library of Congress Control Number: 2021950281

Publisher's Cataloging-in-Publication Data

Names: Abdo, Kenny, author.
Title: Marvel vs. DC: a superhero showdown / by Kenny Abdo.
Other title: a superhero showdown
Description: Minneapolis, Minnesota : Abdo Zoom, 2023 | Series: Versus | Includes online resources and index.
Identifiers: ISBN 9781098228644 (lib. bdg.) | ISBN 9781098229481 (ebook) | ISBN 9781098229900 (Read-to-Me ebook)
Subjects: LCSH: Marvel Comics Group--Juvenile literature. | DC Comics, Inc.--Juvenile literature. | Comic books, strips, etc--Juvenile literature. | Superheroes--Juvenile literature. | Competition--Economic aspects--Juvenile literature.
Classification: DDC 338.7--dc23

TABLE OF CONTENTS

Marvel vs. DC................... 4

The Companies................. 8

Fight! 14

Legacy 18

Glossary 22

Online Resources 23

Index 24

MARVEL vs DC

Few rivalries in history have popped off the pages and into reality quite like the one between Marvel and DC.

The two comic book giants have created some of the most **iconic** heroes of all time. Many, the fans have noticed, weren't exactly original ideas.

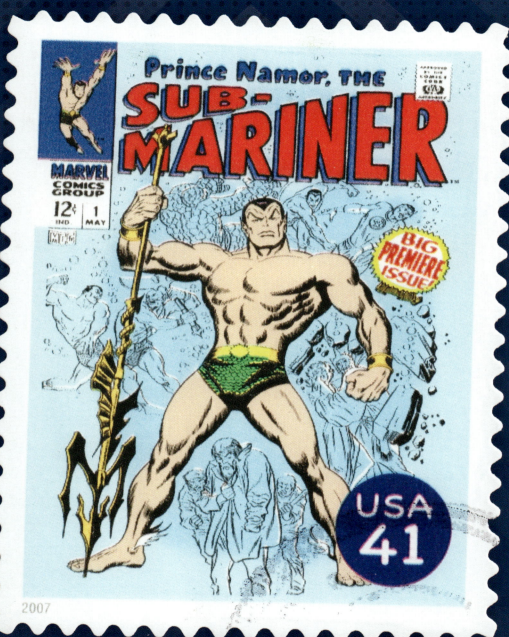

THE COMPANIES

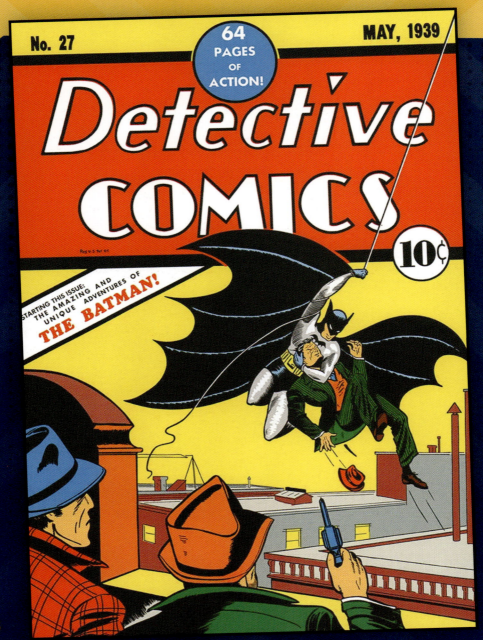

In 1937, Malcolm Wheeler-Nicholson along with Jack Liebowitz founded Detective Comics (DC). By 1938, Superman became a massive hit with *Action Comics* #1.

Magazine publisher Martin Goodman saw the growing popularity of comic books. He created Timely Comics in 1939. The first comic book released by the company was *Marvel Comics #1*.

Timely changed its name to Marvel in 1961. By then, Marvel and DC were already battling. The race to be the first to release the biggest and best heroes was on!

FIGHT!

DC **debuted** Catwoman in 1940. When Marvel's Black Cat leapt onto the scene in the '70s, fans were seeing double. The two feline-inspired burglars wore identical black costumes and had "cat" in their name.

Marvel's Iron Man made his **debut** in 1963. DC introduced Red Rocket in 1987. While Iron Man starred in decades of stories and movies, Red Rocket quickly fizzled out.

DC's Darkseid arrived in 1970. In 1973, Marvel artist Jim Starlin created Thanos. Both characters were giant **demigods** who wanted to destroy the universe, and they also looked nearly identical.

In 2022, DC artist Joëll Jones was accused of **tracing**. Her *Trial of the Amazons* looked exactly like Marvel's *X-Men*. The likeness had fans lighting up Twitter with disappointment.

LEGACY

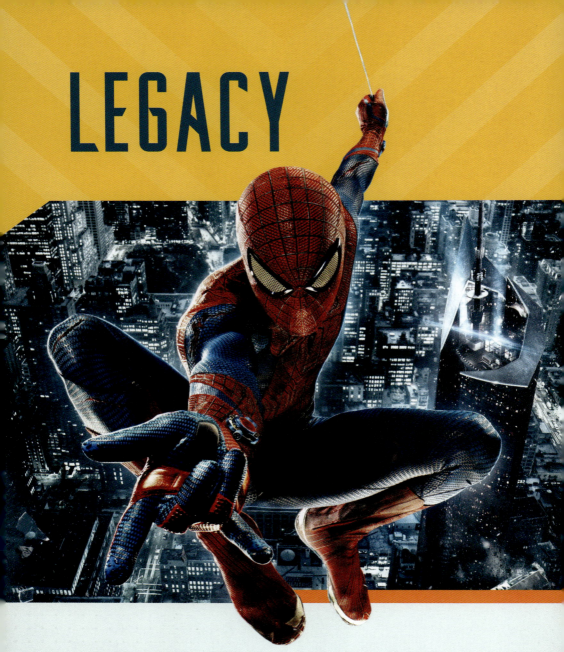

DC and Marvel have duked it out on the big screen too. The movies that star their characters constantly battle for the top of the **box office**.

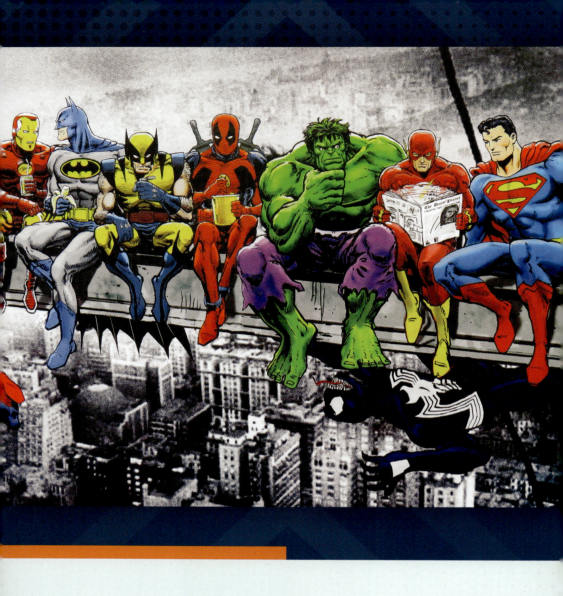

There have been times when Marvel and DC have put their differences aside. Over the years, many **crossover** issues have been released. Like when Superman epically fought Spider-Man.

Marvel and DC continue to be the biggest publishers in comic books. And the heroes they have created remain **pop culture** icons. But the lookalike issues will always remain.

GLOSSARY

box office – used to measure the success of a film by the number of people who go to watch it and the amount of money it makes.

crossover – a series of comics in which characters from one series meet other characters from another series.

debut – appearing in public for the first time.

demigod – a character who is described as half human and half god.

iconic – commonly known for its excellence.

pop culture – popular music, art, literature, fashion, film, or television that is consumed by most of society's population.

tracing – copying a picture or design by drawing over its lines.

ONLINE RESOURCES

To learn more about Marvel and DC, please visit **abdobooklinks.com** or scan this QR code. These links are routinely monitored and updated to provide the most current information available.

INDEX

Action Comics (comic book) 9

Black Cat (character) 14

Catwoman (character) 14

Darkseid (character) 16

Goodman, Martin 11

Iron Man (character) 15

Jones, Joëll 17

Liebowitz, Jack 9

Marvel Comics (comic book) 11

movies 15, 18

Red Rocket (character) 15

Spider-Man (character) 20

Starlin, Jim 16

Superman (character) 20

Thanos (character) 16

Trial of the Amazons (comic book) 17

Wheeler-Nicholson, Malcom 9

X-Men (comic book) 17